Gifted & Talented®

MATH Games

For Ages 6-8

By Vicky Shiotsu
Illustrated by Sean Parkes

LOWELL HOUSE JUVENILE

LOS ANGELES

NTC/Contemporary Publishing Group

Published by Lowell House
A division of NTC/Contemporary Publishing Group, Inc.
4255 West Touhy Avenue, Lincolnwood (Chicago), Illinois 60712 U.S.A.

Managing Director and Publisher: Jack Artenstein
Director of Publishing Services: Rena Copperman
Editorial Director: Brenda Pope-Ostrow
Director of Art Production: Bret Perry
Senior Educational Editor: Linda Gorman
Designer: Carolyn Wendt

Lowell House books can be purchased at special discounts
when ordered in bulk for premiums and special sales.
Please contact Customer Service at:
NTC/Contemporary Publishing Group
4255 W. Touhy Avenue
Lincolnwood, IL 60712
1-800-323-4900

Printed and bound in the United States of America

Library of Congress Catalog Card Number: 00-130070

ISBN: 0-7373-0483-9

ML 10 9 8 7 6 5 4 3 2

NOTE TO PARENTS

Teach a child facts and you give her knowledge. Teach her to think and you give her wisdom. This is the principle behind the entire series of *Gifted & Talented®* materials. And this is the reason that thinking skills are being stressed in classrooms throughout the country.

Gifted & Talented® Math Games has been designed specifically to promote the development of critical and creative thinking skills. The problems in this exciting book include visual puzzles, logic problems, riddles, and more! All the problems will spark children's imaginations, sharpen their thinking skills, and foster a love of learning!

The inviting artwork on each page contains clues to some of the answers and provides visual reinforcement for learning. Some of the problems have been grouped so that they give the child practice using a certain type of thinking strategy. For example, two logic problems may be placed side by side so that when the child figures out how to solve the first one, he or she may apply those skills in solving the second one. Each problem, however, can stand alone, and the problems do not have to be done in any particular order.

Your child may be inspired by the problems in this book to create his or her own puzzles! If so, have your child present the problem to you and explain the answer. Praise your child's efforts, and encourage him or her to continue making more puzzles. This type of activity not only stimulates creativity, but it also develops your child's ability to apply different strategies for solving problems.

TIME SPENT TOGETHER

The time you spend with your child as he or she learns is invaluable. This "one-on-one" contact with your child cannot be duplicated at school. The more positive and constructive an environment you can create, the better. Here are some tips to keep in mind as you work with your child:

- Let your child look through the book and choose the problems that interest him or her. The problems in the book are self-contained and do not have to be done sequentially.

- Allow your child to go at his or her own pace. If your child wants to do only one or two pages, accept that and return to the material at another time.

- Give your child time to think about the answers. A common mistake parents and teachers make is to jump in with the answer when a child hesitates. Help your child by rephrasing the question if necessary, or by providing hints or prompts.

- Remember that your child's level of participation will vary at different times. Sometimes a response may be brief and simplistic; at other times, a response may be elaborate and creative. Allow room for both.

- Offer your child praise and encouragement frequently. It is much easier for a child to learn in a secure, accepting environment.

This book will not only teach your child about many things, but it will teach *you* a lot about your child! Make the most of your time together— and have fun!

ALL IN THE FAMILY

Joe's dad is three times older than Joe. Joe's grandfather is twice as old as Joe's dad. The sum of all their ages is 100. How old is Joe, his dad, and his grandfather?

HERE COMES THE CIRCUS!

Sara was counting the clowns and elephants in the circus parade. She counted 15 heads and 40 feet. How many clowns and elephants were in the parade?

HEADS AND TAILS

Lay four pennies in a row so that the two on the left are heads up and the two on the right are tails up.

Now make three moves, turning over two coins each move. See if you can end up with the two pennies on the left being tails up and the two pennies on the right being heads up. (Do not switch the positions of the coins at any time.)

FISHY SQUARES

How many squares can you see in the fish?

COWS ON THE MOVE

Marty watched some cows walk across a field. First he saw one cow walk in front of two cows. Then he saw one cow walk between two cows. Finally he saw one cow walk behind two cows. How many cows were walking across the field?

"X" MARKS THE SPOT

Lay out 10 pennies in two rows to match the picture below.

Move one coin so that the 10 pennies form an **X** that looks symmetrical. (**Symmetrical** means that one half of something looks the same as the other half.)

IZZY'S PUZZLE

Izzy has just finished painting the block below. When the paint dries, he is going to cut it into nine cubes. Think about what each cube will look like. Then answer the questions.

How many cubes will have four sides painted?

How many cubes will have three sides painted?

How many cubes will have two sides painted?

LIZZY'S PUZZLE

Lizzy painted the big cube below.
Now she is going to cut it into
27 small cubes. Think about
what each small cube will look
like. Then answer the questions.

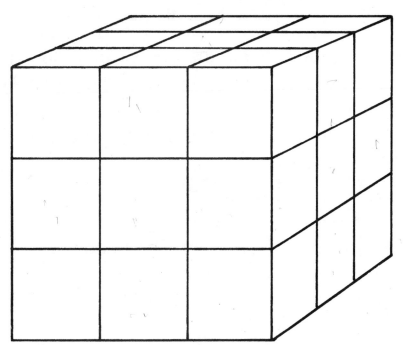

How many cubes will have three sides painted?

How many cubes will have two sides painted?

How many cubes will have one side painted?

How many cubes will have no sides painted?

TRICKY SUMS

On a sheet of paper, draw a three-by-three grid like the one below.

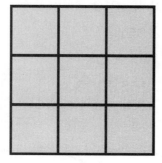

Write the numbers 1 to 9 in the grid so that the sum of the three numbers in any row or column is the same. Use each number only once.

Hint: Rows go across. Columns go up and down.

MAKING PUNCH

Ruby is making a bowl of punch. She needs 7 cups of water. Ruby doesn't have a measuring cup, but she has three pitchers. One pitcher holds 9 cups of water. Another pitcher  holds 6 cups of water. The last pitcher holds 4 cups of water. How can Ruby measure 7 cups of water with her pitchers?

FLIP-FLOP NUMBERS

Look at these numbers.

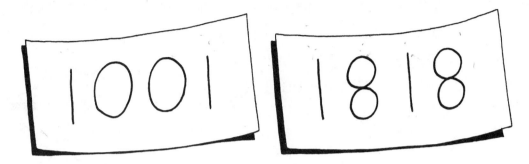

1. What do you think the numbers will look like when you turn this page upside down? Take a guess. Then try it and see!

2. Look at the numbers right-side up again. What do you think the numbers will look like when you turn this page upside down and hold it up to a mirror? Guess first. Then stand in front of a mirror and check your guess!

JENNY'S PARTY

Jenny is having a birthday party at her house this month. See if you can find out when. First, copy the calendar below on a sheet of paper. Then read the clues on the next page. Use your calendar drawing to help you figure out the day of Jenny's party.

Sun	Mon	Tue	Wed	Thur	Fri	Sat
1	2	3	4	5	6	7
8	9	10	11	12	13	14
15	16	17	18	19	20	21
22	23	24	25	26	27	28
29	30					

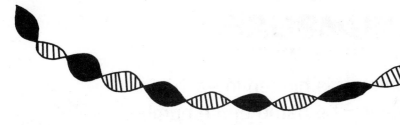

1. Jenny will visit her grandmother on the first Saturday of the month. She will stay at her grandmother's house for three days.

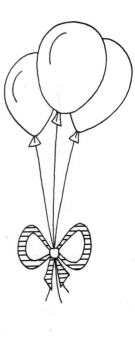

2. Jenny has a dentist appointment on the second Friday. She will not be able to see her friends that day.

3. Jenny always keeps the first and last Sunday of each month open for baby-sitting.

4. Jenny and her parents are going hiking on the third Saturday. They will be out all day.

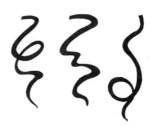

5. The party is not on an even-numbered day.

6. There is no school the day after the party.

HIDDEN NUMBERS

The name of a number is hidden in each of the sentences below. The name of the number in the first sentence has been underlined so that it is easy to see. Find the hidden numbers in the rest of the sentences.

A. I will g<u>o ne</u>xt door to visit my friend. (one)

B. Let's ride a sleigh today.

C. The boy wrote notes to his friends.

D. Matt won a great prize!

E. My dog likes to sniff our shoes.

F. Dr. Rossi x-rays people at the hospital.

G. The marsh was filled with reeds.

H. Mom put a bun in every bag.

I. I'll see if I've got your book.

J. Jan roller-skates even when it rains.

FROM 1 TO 100

Suppose you wrote all the numbers from 1 to 100. Which digit do you think would appear the most? Which digit do you think would appear the least? Take a guess. Then check your answer.

WHAT'S IN LUCY'S PURSE?

Lucy has some money in her purse. She has two bills and seven coins. Lucy has $3.10 all together. Can you figure out what bills and coins are in Lucy's purse?

LOOK-ALIKE FLAGS

These flags may look the same, but they're not! Can you find five differences?

ADD THEM UP!

Copy the circles and lines below on a sheet of paper. Write the numbers 1 to 6 in the circles so that the three numbers along each side of the triangle have the same sum.

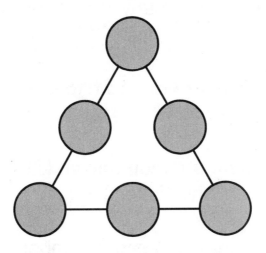

ODD SHAPE

Look at the shapes. Which one doesn't belong?

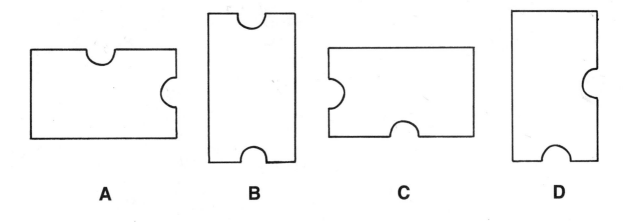

A   B   C   D

FLUFFY'S KITTENS

Fluffy has seven kittens. Each one is a solid color. The kittens are brown, gray, white, or black. Read the clues. Figure out how many kittens of each color Fluffy has.

There are more white kittens than gray kittens.

There are more brown kittens than white kittens.

There is the same number of black kittens and gray kittens.

NUMBER PATTERNS

Look at the rows of numbers.
Each row has its own pattern. See
if you can figure out the patterns.
Then name the two numbers that
are missing in each row.

A. 11, 22, 33, 44, 55, 66, __?__ , __?__

B. 12, 23, 34, 45, 56, __?__ , __?__

C. 1, 4, 7, 10, 13, __?__ , __?__

D. 1, 4, 3, 6, 5, 8, 7, __?__ , __?__

E. 1, 0, 2, 1, 3, 2, 4, 3, 5, __?__ , __?__

F. 1, 4, 9, 16, 25, __?__ , __?__

TAKING AIM

Hannah is trying to get a score of 40. She has four arrows. Each arrow must hit a different number. What numbers should Hannah aim at to get exactly 40?

HOW FAR AWAY?

Look at the points of the triangles. Is B closer to A or C?

PROFESSOR MATHO'S NUMBERS

Professor Matho has six numbered balls. See if you can help him out.

I NEED TO PUT THE NUMBERS IN GROUPS OF THREE. THE SUM OF ONE GROUP MUST EQUAL THE SUM OF THE OTHER GROUP. HOW SHOULD I ARRANGE THE NUMBERS?

PLAYING WITH MARBLES

Millie, Billy, and Tillie are playing with their marbles. They have 14 marbles all together. Millie has twice as many marbles as Billy. Billy has twice as many marbles as Tillie. How many marbles does each child have?

CHICKENS AND EGGS

Three chickens lay six eggs in three days. How many eggs will six chickens lay in six days?

ODDS AND EVENS

Here are some problems with odd and even numbers. Can you solve them? (Do not use the number 0 in your answers. Do not use a number more than once in each answer.)

A. Which three odd numbers add up to 11?

$$\boxed{?} + \boxed{?} + \boxed{?} = 11$$

B. Which three even numbers add up to 14?

$$\boxed{?} + \boxed{?} + \boxed{?} = 14$$

C. Which two odd numbers and two even numbers add up to 10?

$$\boxed{?} + \boxed{?} + \boxed{?} + \boxed{?} = 10$$

D. Which three odd numbers and one even number add up to 11?

$$\boxed{?} + \boxed{?} + \boxed{?} + \boxed{?} = 11$$

A BALANCING ACT

Look at each scale. The weight on one side balances the weight on the other side.

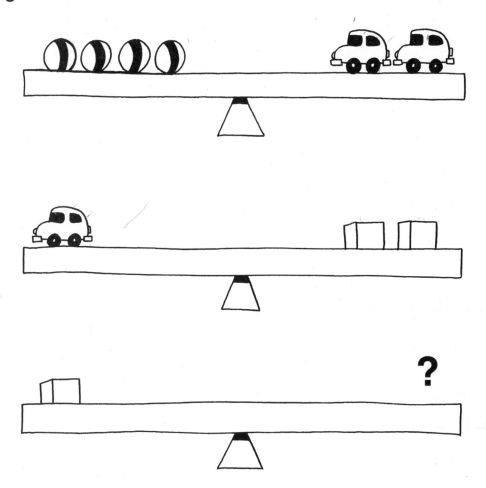

What is needed to balance the last scale?

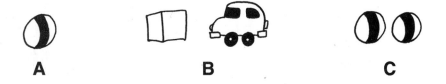

A   B   C

COUNT THE TRIANGLES

How many triangles can you find in the picture below?

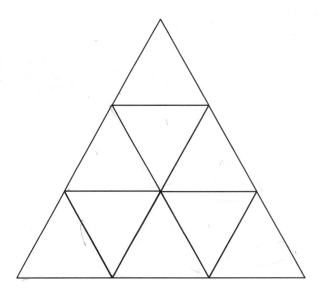

WHAT'S NEXT?

Brad made a pattern with pennies. Look at the pattern. How many pennies will Brad need to create the next set in the pattern?

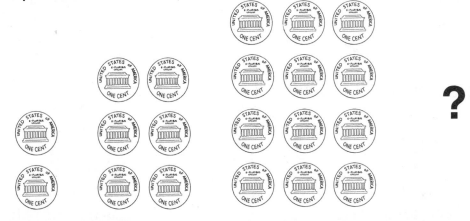

TWO GROUPS OF SUMS

Get a straw. Place it on the page to divide the numbers into two groups. Each group must have the same amount of numbers. The sum of the numbers in each group must be the same.

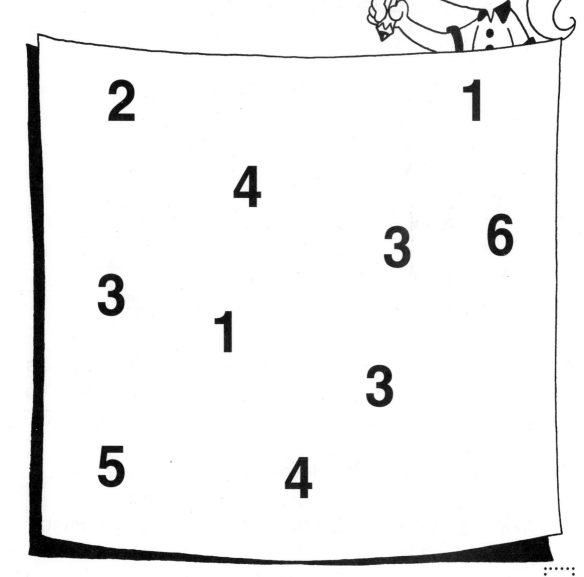

GOING UP AND DOWN

The elevator in Wendy's apartment building is busy going up and down all day long. Read about the people who ride the elevator. Then solve the problems.

A. The Lang family got on an empty elevator. Then twice as many more people got on. Now there are nine people on the elevator. How many members are in the Lang family?

B. Five people got on the elevator on the first floor. Then every floor after that, one person got on while two people got off. At which floor was there only one person left riding the elevator?

C. Mrs. Parker left her apartment and got on the elevator. She went up three floors to visit Mrs. Kelly. Then she went down two floors to visit Mrs. Santos. Mrs. Santos lives on the third floor. On what floor does Mrs. Parker live?

D. Ten people got on an empty elevator on the first floor. As the elevator went up, two people got off on every odd-numbered floor and one person got off on every even-numbered floor. On which floor did the last person get off?

CUT-UP CIRCLE

Alina drew a shape in the middle
of a paper circle. Then she cut the
circle into four equal pieces.

Imagine that you put the pieces back together again. What
shape would be in the middle of the circle?

A CARNIVAL RIDE

Jeff, Max, Fred, and Dan are at the carnival. They are riding on the roller coaster. Two boys are sitting in the back seat and two are sitting in the front. Read the clues and see if you can guess who's who.

Dan is not sitting next to Max.

Jeff and Max are not sitting beside each other.

Fred is sitting in front of Jeff.

Dan is sitting on Jeff's right.

NUMBER TRIOS

Professor Matho arranged some numbered balls in groups of three. Look carefully at the groups. What number should go on the last ball?

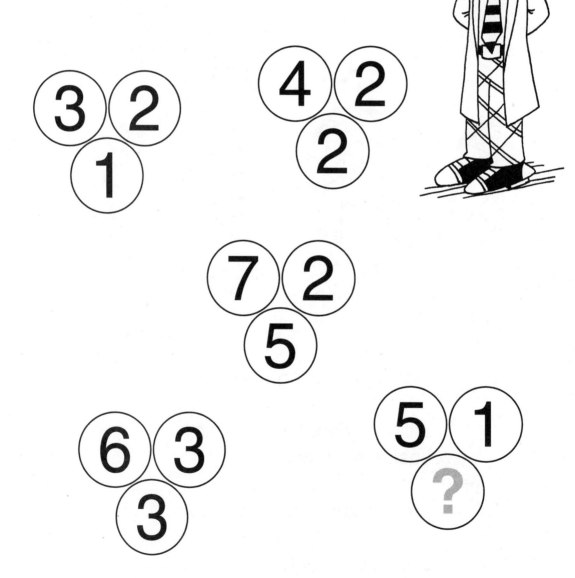

PENCIL PETE'S CHALLENGE

LOOK AT THE PICTURES BELOW. SEE IF YOU CAN COPY THEM ON A SHEET OF PAPER. DRAW EACH PICTURE WITHOUT LIFTING YOUR PENCIL FROM THE PAPER AND WITHOUT GOING OVER ANY LINES TWICE!

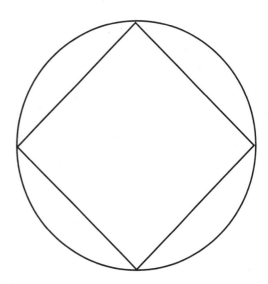

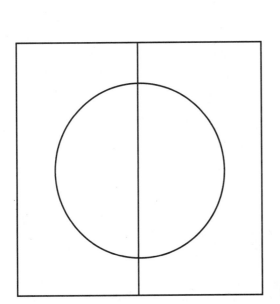

ALMOST PARTY TIME!

Kirsten has invited some friends over for a party at her house. At lunchtime, she still had six hours before her friends would arrive. Read the sentences on the next page to see how Kirsten spent her time. Then figure out how much time she has left before her guests arrive.

PIN THE TAIL ON THE DONKEY

BALLOONS

Kirsten took 15 minutes to eat lunch.

Kirsten and her mom went grocery shopping for an hour.

Kirsten spent half an hour at the party store getting balloons and decorations.

It took Kirsten 30 minutes to clean up the house.

Kirsten and her dad decorated the house in one hour.

It took Kirsten and her parents 60 minutes to prepare all the food.

Kirsten spent a quarter of an hour setting the table.

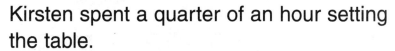

THE FROG IN THE WELL

A frog fell into a well that was 5 feet deep. To get out, he made one big leap every day. He would jump up 3 feet, but then fall back down 2 feet. How many days did it take the frog to get out of the well?

WHAT'S THE NAME?

This boy cut out paper shapes and arranged them to form his name. Can you guess the boy's name?

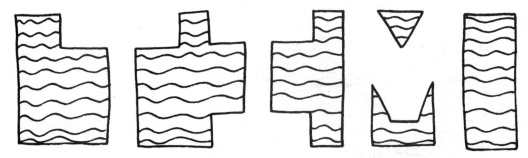

LINES AND SHAPES

Get a pencil and some paper. Then try these drawing activities.

A. Draw a square using four lines. Was that easy? Now draw two squares using only five lines!

B. Draw two squares using six lines.

C. Draw a triangle using three lines. Then draw two triangles using four lines!

D. Draw two triangles using five lines.

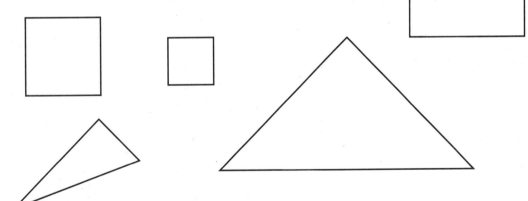

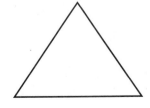

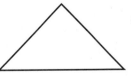

LOOK-ALIKE GLOVES

Look at these gloves. Which one is different?

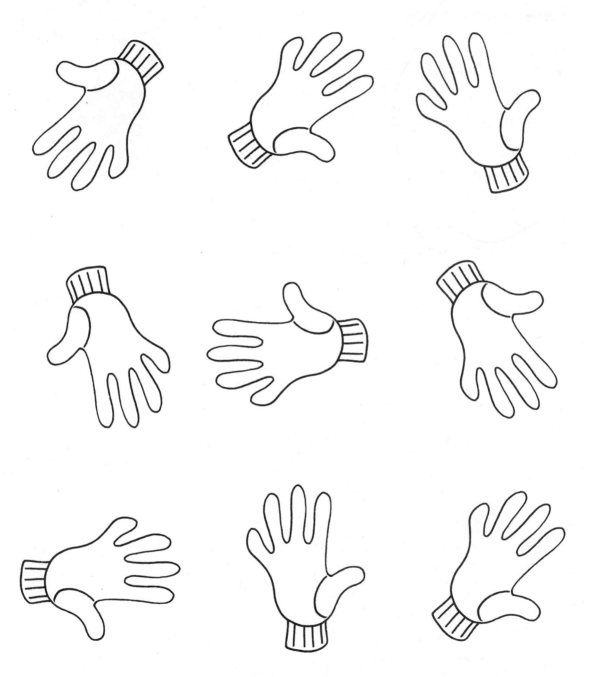

WHAT'S THE SHAPE?

Lindsay cut a paper shape into three pieces. Here are the pieces she got.

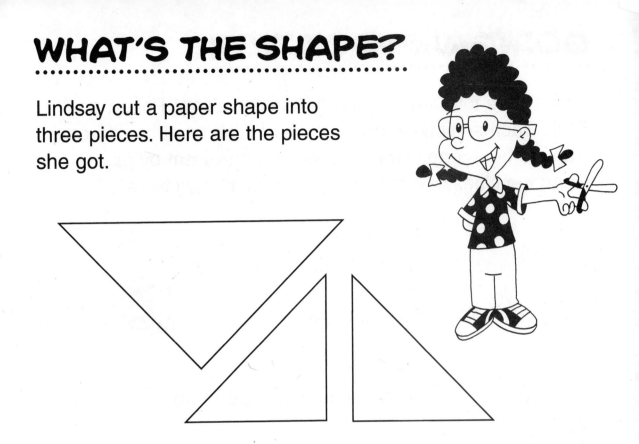

What did the paper shape look like before Lindsay cut it?

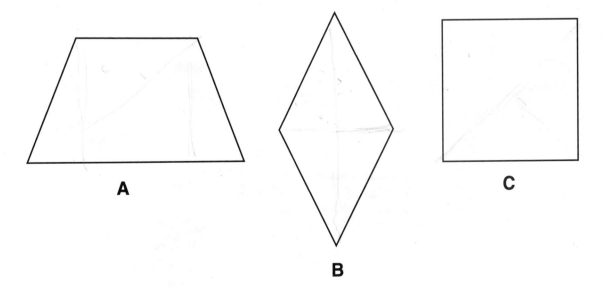

A

B

C

GOING ON VACATION

There were four snails named Peewee, Slimy, Pokey, and Slick. Each snail went on a vacation. One went by car, one went by boat, one went by train, and one went by plane. Read the clues and figure out how each snail traveled.

Peewee and Slimy are afraid of flying.

Slick gets seasick.

Pokey had to stop for gas several times during the trip.

Peewee didn't travel by land.

MATH RIDDLES

These riddles are just for laughs!

A. Seven is an odd number. What can you do to make seven even? (You may not add or take away any number from it.)

B. What is in a line but not in a circle? _____

C. What do you have when you take 10 pennies away from 100 pennies?

D. How can you show that half of 8 is 3?

E. Mr. Jones had three piles of leaves in the front yard. He had two piles of leaves in the backyard. How many piles of leaves did Mr. Jones have when he put the piles together?

MICE AND CHEESE

Get a straw. Place it on the next page to divide the mice and cheese into two groups. Follow these rules:

Each group must have the same number of mice.

Each group must have the same number of cheese wedges.

In each group, there must be the same number of mice as there are cheese wedges.

A NUMBER PYRAMID

Look at the number pyramid. The numbers form a pattern. What number is missing from the pyramid?

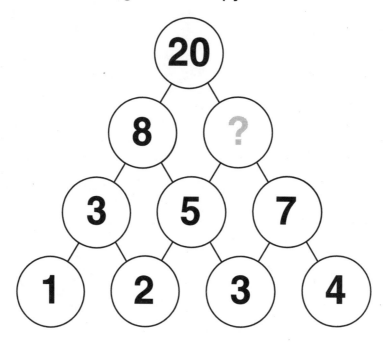

APPLE-PICKING TIME

Some workers were picking apples and putting them into a huge basket. The number of apples in the basket doubled every minute. The basket was full at the end of one hour. When was the basket half full?

THREE TREES

There are three trees growing in front of Greenville School. Read the clues. See if you can figure out their ages.

The youngest tree is 10 years younger than the middle tree.

The middle tree is 10 years younger than the oldest tree.

The youngest tree's age and the middle tree's age add up to 20.

MUFFINS FOR SALE

A baker had some muffins for sale. He sold half of the muffins to his first customer. Then he sold half of the muffins that were left to his second customer. Finally, he sold half of what was left to his third customer. The baker was left with three muffins. How many muffins did he have to begin with?

WHAT DID IT COST?

Angela bought a pencil and an eraser. Together they cost $1.20. The pencil was exactly one dollar more than the eraser. How much did the pencil cost?

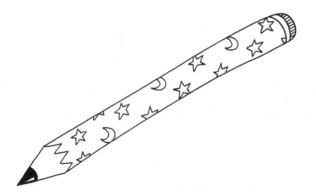

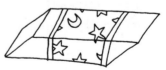

WHAT DOES THE DOG WEIGH?

Sherman wanted to find out how much his dog weighed. When Sherman put his dog on the scale, he found out that it weighed 10 pounds plus half its weight. How much did the dog weigh?

A BIG FAMILY

Seven sisters lived with their parents in a huge house in the country. Each sister had two brothers. How many people lived in the house?

SHAPE GRID

Copy the grid and the shapes below on a sheet of paper. Then follow the directions on the next page.

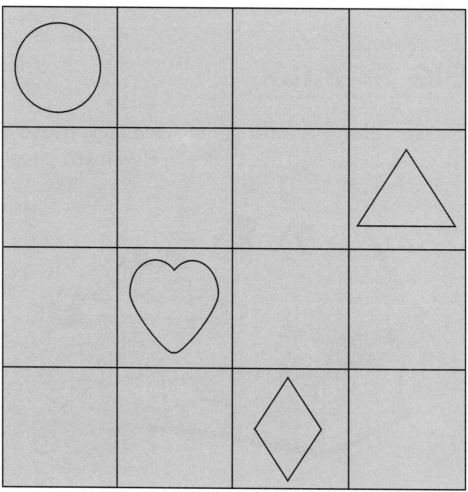

Fill in the grid by drawing circles, hearts, diamonds, and triangles. You must follow these rules:

1. No shape may appear twice in a *row*.

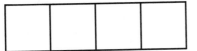

2. No shape may appear twice in a *column*.

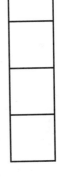

3. No shape may appear twice in a *diagonal row* that goes from corner to corner.

GOOD LUCK!

"EYE" SEE

Look at lines A and B in the shapes below.

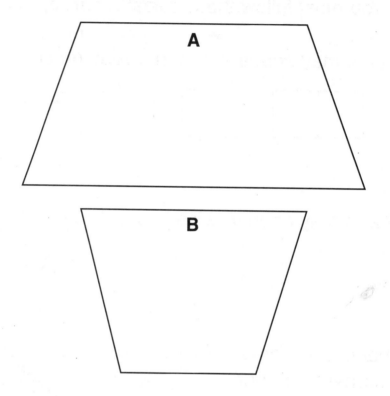

Which sentence is true?

1. A is longer than B.

2. A is shorter than B.

3. A and B are the same length.

After making your guess, measure the two lines to check your answer.

NUMBER WORDS

Tyler started writing number words on a long sheet of paper. He began with **one**. Then he wrote **two, three, four,** and so on. Tyler kept writing the words until he found one that had the letter **a** in it. He wrote that word and then stopped. "I'm finally finished!" he said.

What number word was last on Tyler's list?

ROWS AND ROWS

Get nine pennies. Can you line them up so that you have eight rows of three pennies?

DIVIDE THE RECTANGLE

Suppose you were going to cut the rectangle below in half. Suppose you could only cut along the lines. How many different ways could you cut the rectangle?

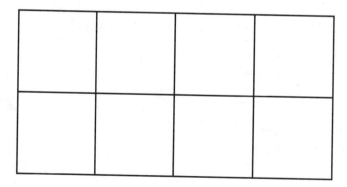

SUPERMOTHERS!

A mother hamster gave birth to seven babies every other month. A mother mouse gave birth to four babies every month. At the end of one year, which mother had more babies?

DOUGHNUT MATH

Tony had a doughnut. He made three cuts to the doughnut to make eight equal-size pieces. How did he do that?

SCHOOL BUS PICKUPS

Mr. Boomer drives a school bus. The bus can carry 55 students. Every school day, Mr. Boomer goes to the first stop and picks up one student. Then he goes to the second stop and picks up two students. He goes to the third stop and picks up three students. If Mr. Boomer keeps picking up one more student at every stop, at which stop will the bus be full?

A TOOTHPICK SQUARE

Arrange eight toothpicks to make a square, as below.

Now add four toothpicks to make four more squares!

MORE TOOTHPICK SQUARES

Arrange 24 toothpicks to make nine squares, as below.

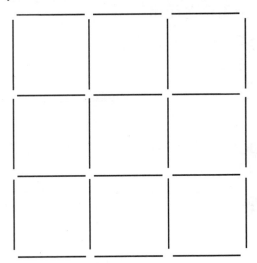

Now take away eight toothpicks so that you have only two squares left!

MEG'S PAPER SHAPE

Meg got a paper square and folded it in half.

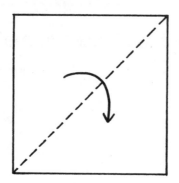

Then Meg folded the paper in half again.

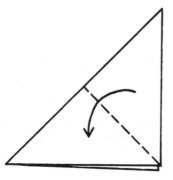

Finally, Meg cut off the point of the paper, as shown.

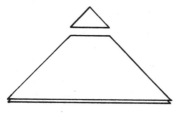

What did the paper look like when Meg unfolded it?

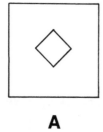

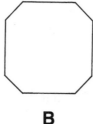

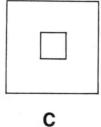

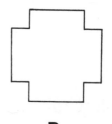

A   **B**   **C**   **D**

GREG'S PAPER SHAPE

Greg got a paper square and folded it in half.

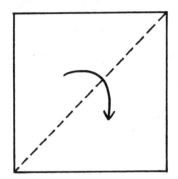

Then Greg folded the paper in half again.

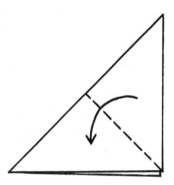

Finally, Greg cut out a V-shape from the point of the paper, as shown.

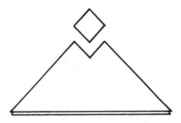

What did the paper look like when Greg unfolded it?

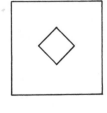   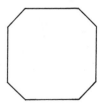   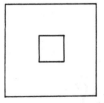   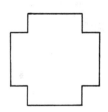

A   B   C   D

FREDDIE FROG'S PATH

Freddie Frog arranged some stones to make a path. Then he painted numbers on the stones. The numbers make a pattern. Look at them carefully. What numbers should go on the last two stones?

CUT THE STRIP

Suppose you had a strip of paper that was divided into 15 squares.

Now suppose you wanted to cut the squares along the strip. If it takes you one second to cut each square, how long will it take to cut the entire strip?

PENNIES CHALLENGE

Get six pennies. Can you arrange them so that you have three rows of three pennies each?

LET'S RACE!

Anna, Patty, Mike, and David ran a race. Read the clues. Figure out who came in first, second, third, and fourth.

Patty finished ahead of David.

Mike finished ahead of Anna.

Anna finished behind Patty.

Mike was not first.

Anna was not last.

ANSWERS

Page 5
All in the Family—Joe is 10, his father is 30, and his grandfather is 60.
Here Comes the Circus!— There were 10 clowns and five elephants.

Page 6
Heads and Tails—Several solutions are possible. Here is one:

Setup:

First move:

Second move: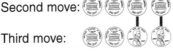

Third move:

Fishy Squares—11 squares: five small squares, five medium-size squares, and one large square

Page 7
Cows on the Move—There were three cows.
"X" Marks the Spot—Pick up the penny at the top right and place it on any other penny to make a symmetrical **X.**

Page 8
Four sides: four cubes
Three sides: four cubes
Two sides: one cube

Page 9
Three sides: eight cubes
Two sides: 12 cubes
One side: six cubes
No sides: one cube

Page 10
Tricky Sums

4	9	2
3	5	7
8	1	6

The sum of each row or column is 15.
Making Punch—Ruby can fill the jug that holds 4 cups. Then she can fill the 9-cup jug and pour the water into the 6-cup jug. When the 6-cup jug is full, there will be 3 cups of water left in the 9-cup jug. The 3 cups and 4 cups make 7 cups.

Page 11
1. The number 1001 stays the same. The number 1818 becomes 8181.
2. Both 1001 and 1818 remain the same.

Pages 12–13
The party is on Friday the 27th.

Page 14
A. I will go next door to visit my friend. – one
B. Let's ride a sleigh today. – eight
C. The boy wrote notes to his friends. – ten
D. Matt won a great prize! – two
E. My dog likes to sniff our shoes. – four
F. Dr. Rossi x-rays people at the hospital. – six
G. The marsh was filled with reeds. – three
H. Mom put a bun in every bag. – nine
I. I'll see if I've got your book. – five
J. Jan roller-skates even when it rains. – seven

Page 15
From 1 to 100—1 appears the most (21 times); 0 appears the least (11 times)
What's in Lucy's Purse?— Two $1 bills, three quarters, three dimes, and one nickel.

Page 16

Page 17
Add Them Up!

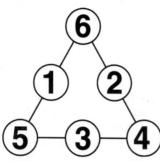

Odd Shape—Shape B, because the rounded cuts in it are on opposite sides. Shapes A, C, and D have rounded cuts on adjacent sides.

Page 18
black—one
gray—one
white—two
brown—three

Page 19
A. 77, 88 (each digit increases by 1)
B. 67, 78 (add 11 each time)
C. 16, 19 (add 3 each time)
D. 10, 9 (add 3, subtract 1)
E. 4, 6 (subtract 1, add 2)
F. 36, 49 (1 × 1, 2 × 2, 3 × 3, and so on)

Page 20
Hannah should aim at 20, 10, 7, and 3.

Page 21
The distance between A and B is the same as the distance between B and C.

Page 22
2, 5, 9 and 3, 6, 7

Page 23
Playing With Marbles—Millie has eight; Billy has four; Tillie has two
Chickens and Eggs—24 eggs

Page 24
A. 1, 3, 7
B. 2, 4, 8
C. 1, 3, 2, 4
D. 1, 3, 5, 2

Page 25
A. one ball

Page 26
Count the Triangles—13 triangles: 9 one-cell triangles, 3 four-cell triangles, and 1 nine-cell triangle
What's Next?—Brad will need 20 pennies to make five rows of four pennies. Each time, the number of rows increases by one and the number of pennies per row increases by one.

Page 27

Pages 28–29
A. three
B. the fifth floor
C. the second floor
D. the eighth floor

Page 30
a square

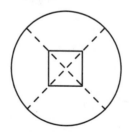

Page 31

	left	right
back seat:	Dan	Jeff
front seat:	Max	Fred

Page 32
The number 4. (In each group, the number on the bottom ball is the difference between the two numbers above it.)

Page 33

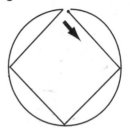

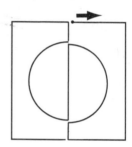

Pages 34–35
Kirsten has 1½ hours until her guests arrive.

Page 36
The Frog in the Well—Three days. On the first day, he leaped 3 feet and fell back 2 feet. He was 1 foot higher in the well, so he had 4 more feet to go. On the second day, he gained another foot, so he had 3 more feet to go. On the third day, he leaped 3 feet and got out of the well.
What's the Name?—The name **TIM** is formed by the white spaces around the shapes.

Page 37

A.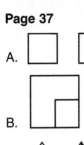

B.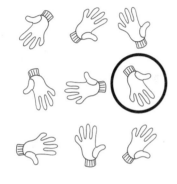

C.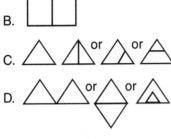

D. (triangles)

Page 38

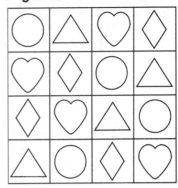

Page 39

C. a square

Page 40

Peewee—boat
Slimy—train
Pokey—car
Slick—plane

Page 41

A. Take the **s** off the word *seven* to get *even*.
B. The letter **n** is in *line* but not in *circle*.
C. 10 pennies
D. Draw a vertical line through the 8 to make the right half "3".
E. one pile

Pages 42–43

Page 44

A Number Pyramid—The missing number is 12. It is the sum of the numbers that are directly below it and connected to it.
Apple-Picking Time—The basket was half full at the end of 59 minutes.

Page 45

The ages of the trees are 5, 15, and 25.

Page 46

Muffins for Sale—24 muffins
What Did It Cost?—The pencil cost $1.10. It is exactly one dollar more than the eraser, which cost 10 cents.

Page 47

What Does the Dog Weigh?—20 pounds
A Big Family—11 people: seven sisters, two brothers, and two parents

Pages 48–49

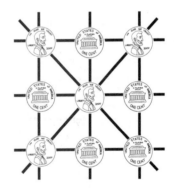

Page 50

Sentence 3 is true.

Page 51

The last number word was *one thousand*.

Page 52

Rows and Rows

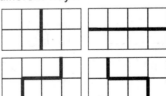

Divide the Rectangle—The rectangle can be cut four different ways:

Page 53

Supermothers!—The mouse had more babies. She had 48 babies, while the hamster had 42.

Doughnut Math

first cut

second and third cuts

Page 54

The bus will be full at the tenth stop.

Page 55

A Toothpick Square

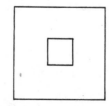

More Toothpick Squares

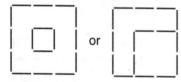 or

Page 56

C.

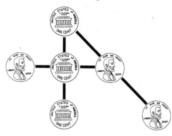

Page 57

A.

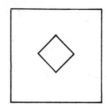

Page 58

The numbers 13 and 21 should go on the last two stones. Each number on the path is the sum of the two numbers before it.

Page 59

Cut the Strip—You would have to make 14 cuts, so it would take 14 seconds.

Pennies Challenge

Page 60

Patty was first, Mike was second, Anna was third, and David was fourth.